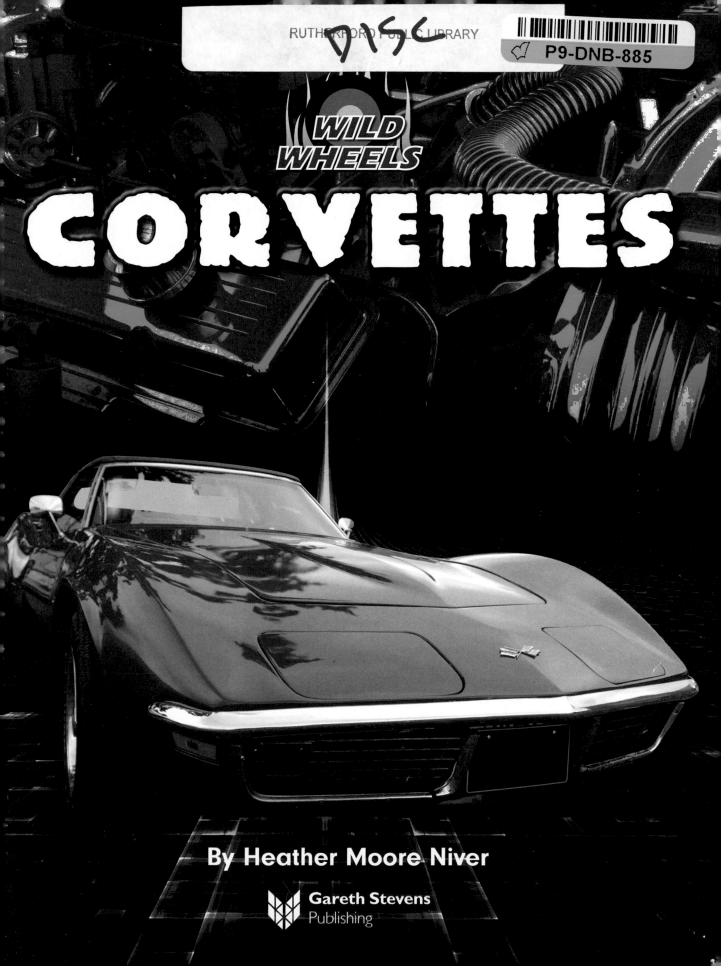

WILD WHEELS

CORVETTES

By Heather Moore Niver

Gareth Stevens
Publishing

Please visit our website, www.garethstevens.com. For a free color catalog of all our high-quality books, call toll free 1-800-542-2595 or fax 1-877-542-2596.

Library of Congress Cataloging-in-Publication Data

Niver, Heather Moore.
Corvettes / Heather Moore Niver.
   p. cm. — (Wild wheels)
Includes bibliographical references and index.
ISBN 978-1-4339-5820-5 (pbk.)
ISBN 978-1-4339-5821-2 (6-pack)
ISBN 978-1-4339-5818-2 (library binding)
1. Corvette automobile—History—Juvenile literature. I. Title.
TL215.C6N58 2011
629.222'2—dc22

2010049266

First Edition

Published in 2012 by
Gareth Stevens Publishing
111 East 14th Street, Suite 349
New York, NY 10003

Copyright © 2012 Gareth Stevens Publishing

Designer: Daniel Hosek
Editor: Kristen Rajczak

Photo credits: Cover, backgrounds (cover and interior pages), pp. 1, 28–29 Shutterstock.com; pp. 4–5, 8–9 JupiterImages/Getty Images; pp. 6–7 Giulio Marcocchi/Getty Images; pp. 9 (inset), 10–11, 12–13, 14 (inset), 14–15, 16–17 Car Culture/Getty Images; pp. 13 (inset), 20–21 Photos.com/Getty Images; pp. 18–19 Ralph Morse/Time & Life Pictures/Getty Images; pp. 22–23 Andrew Sacks/Time & Life Pictures/Getty Images; pp. 24–25 Matt Campbell/AFP/Getty Images; pp. 26–27 Justin Sullivan/Getty Images; p. 27 (inset) Matthew Simmons/Getty Images.

Printed in the United States of America

CPSIA compliance information: Batch #CS11GS: For further information contact Gareth Stevens, New York, New York at 1-800-542-2595.

CONTENTS

Words in the glossary appear in **bold** type the first time they are used in the text.

Cutting-Edge Corvette

The Corvette is a car made by the Chevrolet division of the General Motors (GM) family of cars. On the list of popular sports cars, the Corvette is probably close to the top. This classic car has been made for about 60 years and is known all around the world. As of 2010, Chevrolet had **designed** six generations, or classes, of Corvettes.

A Corvette is sometimes called a 'Vette.

The Corvette started out with only a two-speed **transmission**, but it has become a lean, mean racing machine! Every Corvette model year has its fans. Both old and new Corvettes speed along the highways and star in car shows.

INSIDE THE MACHINE

The Beach Boys' song "Shut Down" features a Corvette racing a Dodge Dart. The cover of their album *Shut Down: Volume 2* shows off a black Corvette Sting Ray.

Creating the Corvette

In the 1950s, GM was one of the biggest companies in the world. They made many cars, but none were like the cool British sports cars Americans wanted to buy. In 1951, Harley Earl was in charge of design at GM. He started to plan a car that would improve Chevrolet's stuffy image.

Even though Earl was only creating a **concept car**, he wanted it to be affordable and to handle like a sports car. This secret design was called "Project Opel." Parts from other Chevrolet models were used in order to keep costs down. The body was made out of lightweight **fiberglass**.

At first, the Corvette was only supposed to be displayed at GM's 1953 New York auto show, Motorama. Then, Chevrolet's chief engineer saw the car. He was excited and knew right away people would want it. GM started making plans to produce the Corvette.

It's said that Chevrolet's chief engineer, Ed Cole, jumped up and down with excitement the first time he saw the 1953 Corvette.

The Very First 'Vette

The first Corvette was beautiful and had a smooth fiberglass body. But it wasn't as speedy as Harley Earl had hoped. It took 11.5 seconds to go from 0 to 60 miles (97 km) per hour. It also wasn't as affordable as planned. Instead, it was the most expensive Chevrolet on the lot!

Car reviewers liked the high speeds Corvettes could maintain on sharp curves. The front **suspension** was made so the car would "stick" to the road when drivers went fast. Drivers didn't have to slow down much on tight curves.

The 1953 Corvette is rare. Chevrolet only made 300.

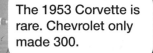

In 1953, Corvette owners didn't get to choose what color their Corvette would be. Corvettes were only made in Polo White with black tops and were red inside. Also, the windows didn't roll down. To get some fresh air while cruising, you'd have to stop and remove the windows!

C1 (1953–1962)

The C1, or first-generation, Corvettes were produced for 10 years. The 1954 Corvettes hadn't changed much from the 1953 model, but drivers could now choose the color of their car. The colors Pennant Blue, Sportsman Red, Polo White, and black were available. In 1955, engineer Zora Arkus-Duntov put an eight-**cylinder**, or V-8, engine under the hood. The Corvette's power, measured in horsepower, increased from 150 to 195 horsepower. The next year, Corvettes boasted 210 horsepower.

Corvettes started to make a profit for GM in 1958.

Chevrolet continued to improve the C1 Corvette. The biggest improvement was the larger V-8 in 1962. C1 Corvettes could now produce between 250 and 340 horsepower!

INSIDE THE MACHINE

Zora Arkus-Duntov is known as the father of the Corvette. Once a European road racer, he joined the Corvette team in 1953. Arkus-Duntov was daring, creative, and inventive. His improvements and fine-tuning kept Corvettes rolling. He even had astronaut Alan Shepard test-drive a model that was still in production!

The Sting Ray Strikes!

The 1963 Corvette was completely different from earlier models. Bill Mitchell, the new chief of design, and Larry Shinoda created a striking body based on the Chevrolet Super Sport. The car had a sleek **prow** and a **fastback**. The rear suspension took up less space and was less expensive. The **coupe** known as the Sting Ray was born.

How was such a dramatically changed car received? Reviewers gave it a big thumbs up! While they loved the way older 'Vettes handled corners, they raved about how the Sting Ray zipped around corners now!

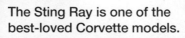

The Sting Ray is one of the best-loved Corvette models.

The 1963 Sting Ray was known as a "split-window coupe." It was designed with a thick bar running down the center of the rear window, splitting it into two parts. It had a stunning appearance, but some thought it was hard to see clearly out the rear window.

split window

C2: Sting Rays (1963–1967)

The C2s had several engine improvements. Engine size and power steadily increased. In 1964, drivers could choose a 365-horsepower engine. In 1965, a large, or big-block, V-8 engine was available. It could create up to 425 horsepower. The 1966 model had an even bigger engine! It was 427 cubic inches (7 L).

Sting Ray engine

The top engine for the 1967 Corvette was the L88. It gave the 'Vette more than 500 horsepower! The L88 was more suited to the racetrack than the street. Many think the '67 Sting Ray is the best Corvette ever made. Today, it's a valuable collectible.

INSIDE THE MACHINE

The 1963 Corvette Sting Ray had a racing option, or choice, known as the Z06. Arkus-Duntov created the Z06 for the racetrack. It had a large gas tank. This helped it compete better in long-distance races because it required fewer stops for refueling.

In 2003, a 1967 Corvette sold for $640,000!

C3: The Mako Shark (1968–1982)

The C3s were based on a concept car called the Mako Shark II that Larry Shinoda designed for the 1965 car show. The 1968 Mako Shark 'Vette had a new flashy shape and finer details. The coupe's roof, called a T-top, had removable panels. The old two-speed transmission was replaced with GM's new three-speed Turbo Hydra-Matic. The C3 was the longest-running Corvette generation.

The third-generation Corvettes were said to be "All Different, All Over."

In 1978, the Corvette celebrated its 25th **anniversary** with two special models. The first was the "Silver Anniversary" edition. It had a two-tone body, silver and gray. The second was a black-and-silver, limited-edition **pace car** for the Indianapolis 500 race.

INSIDE THE MACHINE

The Sting Ray name wasn't completely retired. In 1969, the name returned. This time it was spelled out in chrome script on the front of the car as one word: *Stingray*. The name continued until 1977. Bill Mitchell had used the one-word name for his 1959—1960 race car.

The 1969 AstroVette

In the 1950s, 1960s, and 1970s, US citizens were over the moon about the space program. Mercury, Gemini, and Apollo flights were national events. Alan Shepard, one of the original *Mercury 7* astronauts, loved fast cars. He drove a 1957 Corvette when he joined the space program in 1959.

The *Apollo 12* crew sit on their Corvettes in 1969.

Charles "Pete" Conrad Jr.

Corvette didn't usually give away cars, but for the astronauts they created a special program. Each astronaut was allowed to drive a Corvette, known as an AstroVette, for a year. Shepard and Mercury astronaut Gus Grissom had a friendly rivalry. Each man souped up, or rebuilt, his car in hopes of outperforming the other.

Richard Gordon Jr.

Alan Bean

INSIDE THE MACHINE

The *Apollo 12* crew members all drove matching Corvette coupes. Charles "Pete" Conrad Jr., Richard Gordon Jr., and Alan Bean decided on a special black design. A white line separated black and gold paint, and they had red, white, and blue logos.

C4 (1984-1996)

For the C4 Corvettes, Chevrolet decided to completely redesign the cars instead of just making small changes to the C3s. Just a few C4s were made in 1983, and only one exists today. Chevrolet finally presented the new car in 1984. It was very different from the 1982 Corvette. The inside was roomier, and the instrument display was modernized. T-top roofs were replaced by one piece that could be removed with a wrench.

This 1988 Corvette came in many colors. The most popular was bright red.

Chevrolet fine-tuned the 'Vette through the late 1980s and early 1990s. In 1988, a special 35th anniversary car was issued. It had a white-on-white paint job. For the 40th anniversary, a ruby-red model was issued.

INSIDE THE MACHINE

A bright yellow **convertible** Corvette was the pace car for the Indianapolis 500 in 1986. The car didn't need to be changed at all for the race—it was already fast enough! This was the second time a Corvette had been the race's pace car.

ZR-1: King of the Hill

In 1990, the newest Corvette raced onto the scene: the ZR-1. Nicknamed "King of the Hill," the ZR-1 ruled the road with a V-8 that boasted a jaw-dropping 375 horsepower. Such speed was only possible when the driver set a dashboard key to "full power" mode. In the less exciting "valet" mode, the car had a tamer 250 horsepower. *Motor Trend* magazine found that the ZR-1 could zip from 0 to 60 miles (97 km) per hour in only 4.71 seconds!

Chevrolet still makes the Corvette ZR-1 today.

The ZR-1 wasn't all about speed, though. It was more comfortable and had better **ventilation** than older models. Even the sound system was improved.

INSIDE THE MACHINE

A powerful car like the ZR-1 has to have safety features, just like other cars. The 1990 Corvette included a driver's side airbag and a security system. The ZR-1 had better **antilock brakes** than earlier Corvettes, too.

23

C5 (1997–2004)

C5s were another fresh start for the Corvette. The 1997 'Vette was a **hatchback** coupe with a new engine. The transmission was moved back between the rear wheels to balance the weight of the front engine. Of course, it was fast. *Motor Trend* magazine tested it at 0 to 60 miles (97 km) per hour in 4.8 seconds. The car's 345 horsepower made power-loving drivers happy, too.

In 1998, *Motor Trend* named the Corvette its Car of the Year.

In 1998, a convertible joined the lineup. One option included a special unit that displayed important information, such as speed, on the window. In 2000, a racing version of the C5, the C5-R, won its first victory at the American Le Mans Series race!

INSIDE THE MACHINE

Celebrating 50 years of Corvettes was a big deal to Chevrolet. The 2003 models included an extraspecial 50th Anniversary Edition Corvette. This 'Vette was a deep red and had lots of logos. It was the Indianapolis 500 pace car that year.

C6 (2005-2011)

Instead of remodeling the 2004 Corvette, Chevrolet made careful improvements on the earlier model for the C6. The C6s weren't as long as the C5s. They were leaner and lighter. The 2005 model had a LS2 V-8 engine that produced 400 horsepower and could zip from 0 to 60 miles (97 km) per hour in less than 4.2 seconds!

To increase sales, Chevrolet made some improvements for the 2011 Corvette. One new feature for some of the cars was tires made of "Generation 2" F1 SuperCar rubber made by Goodyear Tires. These tires are made to perform well on wet and dry roads.

The C6 was introduced to the public at the San Francisco International Car Show in 2005.

The C6 was created with another GM car, the Cadillac XLR. The Cadillac inspired some details of the 'Vette, like its interior design and keyless entry.

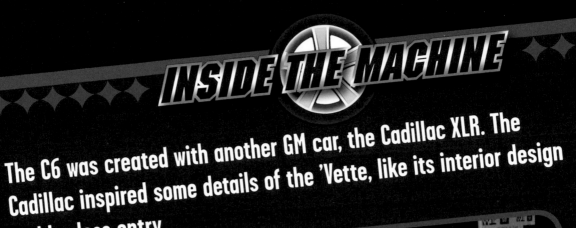

Cadillac XLR

Speeding Ahead

What's ahead for the Corvette? Because of stricter government rules about fuel use, Chevrolet is hard at work developing a new engine. GM must follow these rules, but the company also wants to keep Corvettes as powerful and speedy as ever. The next generation will be the C7.

The Chevrolet Corvette has come a long way from the original two-speed sports car of the early 1950s. Every new generation has improved on the last one and made use of the latest technology. Who knows what roads Chevrolet Corvettes will race down in the future? They're definitely speeding ahead!

A looker like the Corvette was meant for the big screen as well as the road. The Stingray made an eye-catching appearance in the 2009 movie *Transformers: Revenge of the Fallen.* The silver character called Sideswipe was a Stingray.

This silver Corvette is just like the one used in the *Transformers* movie.